Stella McCartney

Queen of the Catwalk

First published in Great Britain in 2016
by Wayland

Copyright © Wayland, 2016

Editor: Elizabeth Brent

Produced for Wayland by Calcium
All rights reserved
Dewey Number: 746.9'2'092-dc23
ISBN: 978 0 7502 9054 8
Library ebook ISBN: 978 0 7502 9053 1
10 9 8 7 6 5 4 3 2 1

Wayland
An imprint of
Hachette Children's Group
Part of Hodder & Stoughton
Carmelite House
50 Victoria Embankment
London EC4Y 0DZ

An Hachette UK Company
www.hachette.co.uk

www.hachettechildrens.co.uk

Picture acknowledgements:

Key: b=bottom, t=top, r=right, l=left,
m=middle, bgd=background

Cover: Getty Images: Atsushi Tomura/Stringer (main);
Shutterstock: Alexandra Glen/Featureflash (inset).
Inside: Adidas: 22–23; Corbis: Edie Baskin 24, Bettmann
7, 30b, Rune Hellestad 15, Hulton-Deutsch Collection
8, POOL/Reuters 2, 27, Reuters 12, Andrew Shaw/
Reuters 11, Andrew Winning/Reuters 23; Dreamstime:
Featureflash 4; Getty Images: Jack Guez 16t, Rolls Press/
Popperfoto 9; Shutterstock: DFree 29, Everett Collection
16b, 21, FashionStock.com 10, 13, 30t, Featureflash
1, 26, Alexandra Glen/Featureflash 17, Henry Harris/
Featureflash 5, Simon James 25, Peter Scholz 19,
Paul Smith/Featureflash 14, 18, Andrius Vaicikonis 20;
Wikimedia Commons: Library of Congress 6.

Stella McCartney

Stella McCartney:
A Great British Designer

■ Stella McCartney is one of Britain's top designers, with a global reputation for her stylish and trendsetting fashion. Stella is also well known for her commitment to animal welfare and environmental concerns, and for her refusal to use fur or leather in her designs.

'I WAS ALWAYS THAT KID THAT WANTED TO BE A DESIGNER AND NOW I AM ONE.'

NAME: Stella Nina McCartney

BORN: 13 September 1971

BIRTHPLACE: Lambeth, London

EDUCATION: Bexhill College, East Sussex; Ravensbourne College, London; Central St Martin's School of Art, London

OCCUPATION: Fashion designer

FAMOUS FOR: Fashion design, ethical fashion, campaigning for animal rights, her father, Paul, being a member of The Beatles

LIKES: Spending time with her family

DID YOU KNOW?

Stella's talent and determination have helped her become a famous and well-respected fashion designer. However, born into a famous family, it took a long time before Stella's design flair finally silenced the critics who claimed her success was largely due to her family connections.

Paul and Linda

Stella's father, Paul McCartney, was incredibly famous during the 1960s, and remains so to this day. He was a member of The Beatles, a groundbreaking band of four young men from Liverpool who took the music world by storm.

The Beatles changed the world of music, and went from playing in tiny venues to being mobbed by screaming and adoring fans wherever they went. In 1969, Paul married a young American photographer called Linda Eastman, who he met when she photographed the band.

THE BEATLES IN 1964 WITH PAUL McCARTNEY SECOND FROM THE LEFT.

STELLA ON HER PARENTS:

'THE WAY MY PARENTS BROUGHT ME UP TO SEE THE WORLD IS STILL ABSOLUTELY KEY TO WHAT I AM ABOUT.'

In 1970, The Beatles broke up and Paul went on to form a new band, called Wings. Linda played the keyboard and sang backing vocals in the band. Stella was born two years after The Beatles broke up and just as Paul was forming Wings. According to him, Wings took its name from Stella's birth, which was difficult. Paul sat outside the operating room, praying that his baby daughter would be born on the wings of an angel.

LINDA AND PAUL McCARTNEY WITH DAUGHTERS (L TO R) HEATHER, STELLA AND MARY.

DESIGN SUCCESS

The McCartney family is large. Stella has an older half-sister, Heather, an older sister called Mary and a younger brother called James. She also has a much younger half-sister called Beatrice.

Rock Family

Having parents in a successful band doesn't lead to the most conventional family life! Bands travel the world to promote albums and play different venues, and Wings were no exception.

Rather than spend time apart, Paul and Linda decided that the whole family would go on tour – wherever in the world that was. Until the age of nine, Stella's life was mainly spent with her family on tour with Wings, travelling to wherever they were performing next.

PAUL AND LINDA McCARTNEY WITH THEIR BAND, WINGS, IN 1971.

In the band's early days, Wings travelled to British universities to perform. They often booked into a bed and breakfast, and improvised a cot for baby Stella from a drawer and sheets! However, as the band became more successful and well known, Wings, and the McCartney children, began to travel the world in greater style.

DESIGN SUCCESS

The McCartney family travelled on a customised British Aircraft Corporation 1-11 jet. It was fitted with a mini-disco with fluorescent lights, luminous stars and a state-of-the-art sound system. The children loved it!

Despite their jet-set lifestyle, Linda and Paul insisted that their children's homelife was as normal as possible. The couple were determined not to spoil their children and to bring them up to realise the importance of hard work.

Paul and Linda didn't want to send their children to an exclusive private school, and instead chose to send them to state schools, like other local children. However, when they were on tour, a private tutor was employed to teach the children so they didn't fall behind with their education.

PAUL McCARTNEY ON HIS CHILDREN'S HOMELIFE:

'IN OUR MINDS, WE WERE GIVING THE KIDS A NORMAL UPBRINGING. WHILE AT THE SAME TIME, WE KNEW IT WAS NOT.'

By the time Stella was ten years old, Wings were no longer together and the McCartney family settled in a farmhouse in Sussex. There, they raised sheep, rode horses, and grew organic produce.

However, the celebrity lifestyle was never far away as Paul carried on working as a successful composer and performer.

STELLA WITH PAUL AND LINDA McCARTNEY IN 1976.

Finding Fashion

From a young age, Stella was fascinated by clothes and fashion, and she loved to dress up in her mum's clothes. By the age of 13, she had made her own jacket and in 1986, 15-year-old Stella arranged to do some work experience in Paris with the prestigious designer Christian Lacroix. Stella now knew she wanted to work in fashion.

A MODEL SHOWS OFF LACROIX DESIGNS ON THE CATWALK.

STELLA ON HER UPBRINGING:

'MY MUM AND DAD HAD CREATIVE JOBS, BUT OUR FAMILY WAS A WORKING FAMILY – SO THERE WASN'T AN OPTION OF "OH, WHEN YOU'RE OLDER, YOU'RE NOT GOING TO HAVE TO WORK."'

When she left school, Stella took up a place on an Art Foundation course at Ravensbourne College, in London. She then studied for a degree in fashion design at the prestigious Central St Martin's School of Art, also in London.

While studying at St Martin's, Stella decided to work as an apprentice to well-respected tailor, Edward Sexton. He made bespoke suits, each one individually made and fitted for the customer. Stella wanted to learn more about the technique and craft of tailoring.

Stella's final show at St Martin's attracted more attention than most students'. This was largely because the models in her show were incredibly famous. The line-up included friends and supermodels Kate Moss and Naomi Campbell. With such a star-studded cast modelling her clothes, the press flocked to Stella's show. It was a hit and her entire collection was immediately bought by a London boutique called Tokio. However, some other students complained that the press simply left after Stella's presentation, which meant their designs went unnoticed by the important fashion journalists.

NAOMI CAMPBELL MODELLING ONE OF STELLA'S DESIGNS FROM HER FINAL SHOW AT ST MARTIN'S.

DESIGN SUCCESS

Following the St Martin's show, there was criticism that the young designer was only receiving attention because of her famous connections, rather than for the quality of her designs. It would take a long time before Stella was acknowledged as a designer whose success was due to her talent rather than the influence and connections of her famous father.

Making Chloé Cool

After leaving Central St Martin's, Stella opened a small shop in London selling silk slip dresses, which became her trademark design. The shop developed a good reputation and Stella's clothes were soon selling well.

Mounir Moufarrige, the head of a Parisian fashion house called Chloé, had heard rumours about the young designer. In 1996, he visited Stella's shop. Stella didn't know who he was, but answered his questions about her designs and plans. After the meeting, Moufarrige offered Stella a job. He wanted her to design clothes that would attract a younger market to Chloé.

'THE GREATEST LUXURY OF HAVING THE PARENTS I HAD WAS THAT ... IN THE BACK OF MY MIND, I ALWAYS KNEW – IF THIS ALL GOES HORRIBLY WRONG, I'LL BE ALL RIGHT. THAT'S AN OPTION THAT MOST PEOPLE JUST DON'T HAVE, FINANCIALLY.'

STELLA IN 1997.

Just two years after leaving St Martin's, Stella was appointed creative director of Chloé. The fashion world was shocked that such a young and inexperienced designer had been given such a key position.

Design Success

Chloé's previous creative director, Karl Lagerfeld, was scathing of Stella's appointment, suggesting it was due to the fame and connections of Paul McCartney rather than the designer's talent.

LAGERFELD IS REPORTED TO HAVE SAID: '[CHLOÉ] SHOULD HAVE TAKEN A BIG NAME. THEY DID, BUT IN MUSIC, NOT FASHION. LET'S HOPE SHE IS AS GIFTED AS HER FATHER.'

A MODEL WALKS THE RUNWAY DURING A CHLOÉ FASHION SHOW IN 2011.

Stella left her London base to work at Chloé in Paris. She went with her close friend Phoebe Philo, from St Martin's. Phoebe was to work as Stella's design assistant.

Solo Stella

Stella worked at Chloé for four years, designing a range of fresh, modern clothes, just as Moufarrige had hoped when he employed her. The appointment was a success: in 2000, Stella won the VH1/Vogue Fashion and Music Designer of the Year Award. She was even commissioned to design the wedding dress for pop star Madonna's high-profile wedding to the actor and director Guy Ritchie.

'CHLOÉ HAS NOT JUST GOTTEN SUBSTANTIALLY BETTER. IT HAS BEEN TRANSFORMED.'
ROBIN GIVHAN, WASHINGTON POST

STELLA AT THE OPENING OF HER FIRST LOS ANGELES STORE IN 2003.

In time, though, Stella decided she wanted to design for her own fashion label, and parted company with Chloé in 2001. She then teamed up with Gucci Group, the company behind the luxury design brand Gucci, to launch her own label. When Stella left Chloé, Phoebe Philo took over the role of creative director.

Stella's first collection for her own label was not a great success. The designs were very different from her usual, more subtle style. Once again, critics began to grumble that the young designer's status was more linked to her famous surname than her talent.

STELLA ADMITTED THAT HER FIRST SHOW AS AN INDEPENDENT DESIGNER WAS A 'MASSIVE MISSTEP'.

'I WAS STILL FINDING MYSELF AS A PERSON AND I WAS TRYING TO FIND MYSELF AS A BRAND TOO QUICKLY. I WAS NERVOUS AND I WAS OVER THINKING THINGS . . .'

KATE HUDSON HAS CHAMPIONED STELLA BY WEARING HER DESIGNS.

DESIGN SUCCESS

Stella's designs have not always worked and there have even been some notable disasters. In 2001, actress and friend Kate Hudson wore one of Stella's dresses to the Oscars and ended up on the Worst Dressed Lists that followed in the media!

Turbulent Times

W hen Stella was 26 and working for Chloé, her much-loved mother Linda died. She was just 57, and had been battling breast cancer for three years. Stella was devastated. Linda had been an inspiration for Stella in both her work and her personal life.

PAUL AND LINDA McCARTNEY IN 1997.

F our years after Linda's death, Paul McCartney married Heather Mills, with whom he had a daughter, Beatrice, in 2003. This relationship caused a rift within the previously close McCartney family, because Paul's children were unhappy about the marriage. Within six years, Paul's second marriage had broken down and a bitter divorce followed. In October 2011, Paul married for a third time, to Nancy Shevell, an American businesswoman.

PAUL McCARTNEY WITH HEATHER IN 2004.

DESIGN SUCCESS

In 2003, Stella married publisher Alasdhair Willis on the remote Scottish island of Bute, in a wedding that featured white roses, a bagpipe band and fireworks. Today, the couple live with their four children, Miller, Bailey, Beckett and Reiley, in London. At weekends, they often go to their house in Wiltshire.

ALASDHAIR SAYS: 'WE ARE HAPPY. WE RESPECT EACH OTHER, WE ENJOY EACH OTHER'S COMPANY AND SHE'S MY BEST FRIEND. I LOVE HANGING OUT WITH HER.'

Today, Stella and her father are once again close friends. Paul is often seen sitting proudly in the front row at her fashion shows!

Once Stella was known as the daughter of a famous father. Today, Paul says he is often known as the father of a famous fashion designer!

'I'M INCREDIBLY SAD THAT MY MOTHER'S NOT HERE TO SEE MY KIDS AND THAT MY KIDS DON'T GET TO KNOW HER. AND SHE DIDN'T MEET MY HUSBAND. THAT'S ONE OF THE HARDEST THINGS. I DON'T EVEN KNOW HOW TO PUT THAT INTO WORDS.'

Becoming a Brand

Despite the rocky start, Stella's own label soon became a respected and successful brand. Under her own brand name, Stella opened a store in New York in 2002. She now has more than 30 of her own stores in key fashion cities throughout the world, including London, Milan, New York, Paris and Tokyo, and sells her collections in over 600 other stores. Stella's collections include lingerie, accessories, fragrances and children's clothing.

STELLA'S LOS ANGELES STORE.

Stella's apprenticeship with Edward Sexton gave her invaluable tailoring skills, for which her clothes are well known. The designer uses the skills she learnt in her early career to create clothing that is beautifully finished and that fits the wearer perfectly.

STELLA ON HER DESIGNS:

'I WANT THE CLOTHES TO BE MODERN AND COOL .... AND AT THE SAME TIME, THEY HAVE GOT TO BE PERFECTLY CONSTRUCTED IN THE MOST BEAUTIFUL FABRIC, BECAUSE I WANT THEM TO LAST NOT JUST YOUR LIFETIME BUT YOUR DAUGHTER'S LIFETIME AND HER DAUGHTER'S LIFETIME.'

In 2005, Stella designed a range of more affordable clothes for high street fashion store H&M. The collection featured Stella's trademark trousers, blazers, blouses and beautiful dresses. The launch was such a success that the clothing range sold out in record time, snapped up by high-street buyers who wanted to add a Stella McCartney piece to their wardrobe.

MODELS PRESENT THE NEW STELLA MCCARTNEY WINTER COLLECTION IN BARCELONA IN 2011.

'I WANT THE WOMAN WHO COMES INTO MY STORE TO FEEL AT EASE, TO SEE A DRESS AND TRY IT ON AND TO LOVE HOW IT MAKES HER FEEL.'

DESIGN SUCCESS

Stella set up a scholarship to fund places at Central St Martin's School of Art on the basis of 'academic excellence and financial need'. The students who win the scholarship places are also offered a one-year paid placement at Stella McCartney, but the designer asks that they agree not to use fur, leather or products that harm animals as part of their work, in line with her firm beliefs.

Green Design

The fashion world is not usually associated with respect for animal rights (many luxury fashion houses use fur), nor for its concern for the environment. Stella McCartney, however, wants to change this.

ERMINES ARE ONE OF A NUMBER OF ANIMALS HUNTED FOR THEIR FUR. THE FUR IS USED TO MAKE CLOTHES IN SOME FASHION HOUSES.

STELLA SPEAKING ABOUT ANIMAL CRUELTY:

'FIFTY MILLION ANIMALS ARE KILLED EVERY YEAR FOR BAGS AND SHOES. EVEN IF YOU'RE NOT INTERESTED IN THE CRUELTY ASPECT, THERE'S A HUGE ENVIRONMENTAL IMPACT. VAST WATER RESOURCES, AND GRAIN THAT COULD OTHERWISE BE GOING INTO PEOPLE'S MOUTHS, ARE GOING THROUGH AN ANIMAL IN ORDER TO BECOME AN ACCESSORY.'

STELLA ON THE ENVIRONMENT:

'I BELIEVE IN CREATING PIECES THAT AREN'T GOING TO GET BURNT, THAT AREN'T GOING TO LANDFILLS, THAT AREN'T GOING TO DAMAGE THE ENVIRONMENT.'

Stella's stores are powered by renewable energy. The wood floors are made from sustainably-managed forests. All of the shoes produced by Stella are made of vinyl or plastic, and all belts and bags are made from raffia and fabric. Fabrics are organic wherever possible. Stella's shoes are even stamped with the words 'suitable for vegetarians.'

Stella does reluctantly use the materials wool and silk. Although sheep are not killed in the process of getting wool, Stella believes that it can still cause them harm. Her company works only with wool suppliers that can prove their sheep are treated in the most humane way possible. Stella admits that she has not yet found an alternative to silk, a material that she believes exploits the silkworm.

KATE HUDSON IS A FAN OF STELLA'S SUITS.

DESIGN SUCCESS

Along with dad Paul and sister Mary, Stella developed the idea of a 'Meat-Free Monday'. The aim of this campaign was to encourage people to eat less meat and to raise awareness of the environmental impact of farming livestock for meat production. A United Nations report in 2006 stated 18 per cent of the world's greenhouse gases are caused by the livestock industry. These gases are having a dramatic and negative effect on the world's climate.

Branching Out

Stella is always keen to develop new ideas and work in new areas. She has designed clothes for the theatre and musicians and has also become involved in designing for sportswear.

In 2004, Stella designed clothes for musicians, including Madonna's Re-Invention tour and Annie Lennox's summer tour. She also designed costumes for the film *Sky Captain and the World of Tomorrow*. In 2011, she designed the clothes for a New York City Ballet production called *Ocean's Kingdom*, the first ballet for which her father, Paul, had written the music.

In 2004, Stella began to work with the sports company, Adidas. The collection, called Adidas by Stella McCartney, has since grown to include a wide range of different sportswear for sports and activities including yoga, tennis, golf and skiing.

In 2010, Stella was proud to be chosen to design the clothes for Team GB's Olympic kit. This was the first time that a high-profile designer had been appointed to this role.

'AS A BRITISH FASHION DESIGNER, IT IS AN AMAZING, ONCE-IN-A-LIFETIME OPPORTUNITY TO BE CREATIVE DIRECTOR OF TEAM GB AS THE HOSTING NATION OF THE LONDON 2012 OLYMPIC GAMES.'

DESIGN SUCCESS

In January 2007, Stella launched an organic skincare line. For this, she refuses to use any ingredients made from genetically modified (GM) materials – that is, plants that have been altered by humans. She also won't use plants that were picked by child labourers or any that are on an endangered species list.

Influences

Stella's designs are centred around her desire to make clothes that are beautiful and wonderful to wear, but that do not cause harm to animals or the environment by their creation. Stella says her determination to build an ethical business is mainly due to the influence of her mother, Linda.

Stella designed her own wedding dress, basing it on the dress Linda wore to her wedding to Paul. Every season, Stella honours her mother with a new shoe design in her memory.

STELLA SPEAKING ABOUT HER MOTHER:

'MY MUM REALLY WAS THE COOLEST CHICK IN THE WORLD.'

STELLA TALKING ABOUT THE INFLUENCE OF HER MOTHER:

'MY MUM HAD A MASSIVE INFLUENCE ON ME, NOT JUST IN WHAT SHE WORE AND HOW SHE LOOKED, BUT IN HER SPIRIT.'

Stella was devastated by her mother's early death. Since then, she has worked with many cancer charities to raise money and to improve awareness of the disease. She designed headscarves to be given free to patients receiving cancer treatment at London's King's College Hospital. The money raised from the sale of the scarves elsewhere, was given directly to the hospital to help with its cancer work.

The loss of her mother to breast cancer made Stella realise how important it is that women know how to check for early signs of the disease, and have access to proper treatment. Stella designed a range of pink underwear for her own brand, and donated the money from sales to the Linda McCartney Centre in Liverpool, where women can be tested and treated for breast cancer.

DESIGN SUCCESS

Stella is involved in a great deal of charity work and many campaigns. She works with People for the Ethical Treatment of Animals (PETA) to inform people about animal rights issues. Recently, she has become involved in a project to raise money for War Child, to support children living in areas of conflict around the world.

Celebrating Success

S tella McCartney's skills and vision as a designer have been recognised throughout the fashion industry and beyond. These are just some of the awards she has received:

2000: VH1/Vogue Fashion and Music Designer of the Year Award for her work at Chloé (presented by her father, Paul).

2007: Designer of the Year at the British Style Awards. On receiving the award, Stella said: 'My team really deserve this. I couldn't possibly manage with three children under the age of three without them.'

2008: Accessories Council Excellence Award for Green Designer of the Year.

2009: Named one of Glamour magazine's Women of the Year.

Included in TIME magazine's list of the 100 most influential people in the world.

Natural Resources Defense Council Award.

2011: British Fashion Council's Red Carpet Award.

2013: Joins list of the 100 most powerful women in Britain, judged by BBC Radio 4's Woman's Hour.

Elle Style Award for Best International Designer of the Year.

H&M & Elle Conscious Award, received for her charity work.